The Man at the Corner Table

superbia in proelio

The Man at the Corner Table

Corner Table
Rosie Shepperd

SEREN

Seren is the book imprint of
Poetry Wales Press Ltd.
57 Nolton Street, Bridgend, Wales, CF31 3AE
www.serenbooks.com
facebook.com/SerenBooks
twitter@SerenBooks

The right of Rosie Shepperd to be identified as
the author of this work has been asserted in accordance
with the Copyright, Designs and Patents Act, 1988.

© Rosie Shepperd 2015
ISBN: 978-1-78172-246-6
e-book: 978-1-78172-248-0
Kindle: 978-1-78172-247-3

A CIP record for this title is available from the British Library.

The publisher acknowledges the financial assistance of the Welsh Books Council.

Book cover artwork: original print by Helen Baines.

Printed in Bembo by Bell & Bain, Glasgow.

Author website:www.rosieshepperd.com

Contents

You all have lied

And now I'm at the stage where
      I see you all the time,
   even places you would never go,
     places I know better than
         to imagine you've taken to swing music,
      succulents, Lebanese food,
        waiting for cabs. Or anything.

The man at the corner table of Al Haram
         hangs his jacket on a teak chair,
      brushes out creases, tugs at the sleeves;
   holds a glass of Hochar just as you did, moves it in a circle,
waits for the light to catch the colour, throw it off
        in triangles of scarlet, plum, sometimes gold;
   smiles at something only he and I know. Or that's the way I see it.

You are here

for PCB

in the creaking clam baskets spread
out in the sun at Po Toi and
what became of the hat shops that lined
small lanes in Macao;

in a particular silver of driftwood that vanishes
into first light and
again in the height of wild garlic that bends
into uncertain shade.

You are an arc of white spine that breaks
at the top of Junk Peak and
there in the green mist of tea that shapes
the air at Lock Cha;

in a deliberate scent of star jasmine as it curls
towards its own weight and
again in a sharp cloud of sand that weaves
the Siberian wind.

You are here in the slope of red roofs that step
from Sai Kung to the sea and
again within freshwater pearls, left
in the palest jade bowl;

in an uncertain shine of black beans entangled
in glass noodle soup and
again in the name for those islands, wrapped
in blue clouds from Lantau.

You are here in the slope of your arm as you turn
into your days and
again in the curve of your face as you unfold
from your house on the hill.

Somewhere I read that a thought can be exaggerated, while an emotion cannot

The chef at Suntory considers sea bream for (maybe) ten seconds.
        He selects yellowfin with absurd red flesh,
      smiles at the silver scales;
          the dark lines on her back
           smile back.

You're late and I flick through *The Trib*, spy a piece on fish scales.
      They grow flat only on skin;
         in the lab they form prisms.
            Beyond any meaningful depth,
    3D is unnecessary and unhelpful.

It's gone again, that so-easy thing we had for each other.

Unwrapping chopsticks takes forever. I reach for the gold hashioki,
        you lean yours against your plate,
      watch as a sous-chef with extraordinary hands
             mixes fine green wasabi with Tokusen;
       folds shavings of pink ginger into tiny glazed bowls.

     Strangers sit opposite us and next to us, and we incline our heads
        together and at each other, bound by this thing,
this art form we're watching. Water chestnuts become flowers, strips
    of squid are stencilled, fanned into a helix of white,
           thrown into clouds of sesame.

Don't worry; the toughest question is not aimed at you.

Parapluie

for P & ZG

I do not want to be made of blue velvet;
I want to be blue velvet. With a handle of silver
shot lace, made by a consumptive old
Romanov who sips her remittance in tall
thin glasses of sweetened black tea.

It is an understatement to say I wish
to shimmer; that I'm quietly reflective
of colour. Selective colour.
I do not want to reflect grey.

I want to be crafted with unprecedented
patience by a slender man who has no
English and fabulous hands. I want to stand
alone, without the icy compromise of a solitary
walk in St Petersburg. I want to lie;

lie beautifully within the fabrication
of my fabric. I want to spread, not just my folds
but myself, on the edge of a shelf of mahogany or
a complex inlay of cherry.

I will be complete but not
undone by a ribbon of magenta. I will be warmed
by dry fired irons and the only creases that fall
from me will be creases that are not
part of the truest part of me.

I will be held by a thin frame of teak, picked
from a clearing in Burma. It has been
rosined with cinnamon and dipped in a resin
of smoked cane sugar.

I will hear the wind before it blows through
the gap in a sash window of a fifth floor
rent-controlled apartment on the west side
of Wenceslas Square. I will contemplate only
the nature of rain.

If I am left in the maze of secondhand shops
that runs under Rue de Rivoli; if I'm thrown on a bonfire
at the end of no particular week, my combustion
will form a distraction of radiance.
I will show you the origin of red.

Ponte Vecchio

Not for the first time, I'm staying in a hotel whose name I don't know.
The voice that said I'd join you in Florence? I'm sure that was mine.
But who's this, in a thin blue silk dress, in the thick part of evening?

A long grilled pepper floats in red juices, crazy with oil and sweet basil.
You lean back to tell me, "These places have so many possibilities."
They might be living their possibilities. Not everything is conditional.

My napkin is a starched square, lovely smelling, in ceramic neatness.
The round half litre of Morellino sits, patient, to the left of my hand.

You excuse yourself to check on something – it could be anything:
Cheese? Tickets for tomorrow? The faltering signal on your phone?

A flat-faced woman passes, with roses wrapped in cellophane tubes.
It's been a while now since I've stopped making regular use of similes.

Balthazar Bakery, Spring Street

Curious how your urge to be up and out of here
supersedes your desire to leave me a note
but as I lie listening to your tip-tap-toeing between
shower   cupboards   dresser   and what I call *loo*
my unwillingness to engage in anything morning-like
with you is overtaken by thoughts of Medialunas and
Galette des Rois down at Balthazar Bakery on Spring Street
where in the miserly hours
we saw men in full-length sky blue aprons
drizzle focaccia and boil bagels and two held
great cream bowls of batter
for hazelnut waffles and buckwheat crêpes and the son François
– dark eyed and already in the street –
lent over to write on the board:

> *Confitures du Jour –*
> *Fraise des Bois*
> *Grenade et Citron Vert*
> *Cerise Noir*

I know he'll smile as I step from the cold in 10 a.m. slingbacks with
my oyster evening coat over uncovered legs and I know he'll enjoy
the colour filling my face and my hands tearing
a tartine and my eyes holding his
over that first Chocolat Chaud.

Listening to music with you in bad weather
is worse

When I remind you that precarious
　　　　is not the same as
　　　　　　　　prodigious and you don't care.

When I look up to see your table
　　　　manners in tatters,
　　　　　　　　like a badly X-rayed tetrapod.

When I overhear you expound
　　　　that tinned sweet corn is
　　　　　　　　one of your five-a-day.

When you twitch your nasal hair
　　　　and ask if I've actually seen
　　　　　　　　Dürer's Hare; when and where.

When you read eco-poetry, dismantle
　　　　the photocopier and complain
　　　　　　　　that too many people complain.

When I discover Coleridge
　　　　preferred codeine and was also
　　　　　　　　a stranger to the bathroom.

When I start to see
　　　　your defining qualities in
　　　　　　　　the anatomy of a coelacanth.

When you become lost for clichés and liaise
　　　　with the leaves at
　　　　　　　　the bottom of your cup.

When I remember that the average
        fighter pilot dies
                    before 25.

When I consider this
        a long time to be flying
                        while dying.

Savoy Hotel, London

Those nights downstairs at the American Bar;
it's not just the chairs that show gilt in the telling.
Back then we were almost quite something.
You and London were lean;
your eyes, a fraction off-centre as you
struggled not to say,
We have this connection. My God.
You overplayed.
And not just your hand.

My role in this mellow
drama was to shift that arse
you loved to chase and twitch my best side
close to the oh-so-Maraschinos.
Too long ago, they were fruit in a tree.
Some tree.
I guess they were something for me
to play with; the pretence
we were ever friends was just
a way to simulate sharing.

30:70 and I never found out
who made the best bet
but I do know that's the wrong word.
Early is just another kind of late and
anyway, you were always
there each night, every night. There's
no fool like a blind
fool; thank God I didn't see the edge
till I was over and out
the other side.

If I buy you a Mojito, will you talk over meter
while I watch how passion fruit slides down a glass?

I'll curl mint in my fingers, squeeze pips from a lemon and scoop
even numbers of cucumber seeds.

You'll consider infusions of spiced Polish vodka and I'll shiver,
though not exclusively for you.

I'll perch at the bar; mock an unsteady rock and by ten, my
stockings will be crossing and if

I'm successful, a dozen sliced limes will simultaneously tremble.

I'll pretend I'm a waitress from Bucharest and stand almost
still at the long silver counter.

I'll wear a white shirt with darts but no pockets and I'll reach
for a soda and nibble a pretzel.

While you're still pouring, my thoughts will come tumbling:
My expiring visa. My fat neighbour's persistence.

The unexplained sourness of nocturnal rain.

After 2 weeks of insomnia I move into the loft with the other pastry chefs

14 days, staring through the scaffold, passing
        Lipton's Lemon to Len, Gerald and Keith.
I climb out there with them, hand up tiles to form
        A short-crust lid over the attic.

Beautiful squares, layered perfect and pale.

Sharing extraordinary patience and a ladle,
        We mix decaff espresso icing,
Winch it up, slopping and very slightly separating
        In a Fortnum & Mason bucket.

We lean against the silence and re-point
        The east wall, our heads nearly touching as we
Listen to egg whites become whiter;
        Drying in shadows on our arms.

The quiet is broken when a few insulation boys
        Poke uncovered heads through a half-done
Dormer, then back to compare their hideous hands.
        Shrugging jalapeño smiles

They wipe barley sugar splinters on their arses.

At 2:00 a.m. my diabetic husband predicts his death

for SP

"It occurs to me from day to day and sometimes from
          minute to minute that I specifically know the
name of the thing that's going to kill me. It's not a Ford
          Focus, a heart attack or an old school chum,
armpit deep in fraud and who (it seems) did not swim
          to Goose Green from the Sheffield. I won't fail
to brake on black ice or allow a small household article to
          become lodged in my gullet. I won't be crushed
by a flip-chart at a symposium on adrenal failure and when
          I emerge from the Odeon, I will avoid the bucket of
butter-corn, ditched by the couple who did not see the whole
          of *The English Patient*. I won't choke on a cashew,
I don't powder-board and do not own a bungee. I won't be
          trapped under Swindon's carbon footprint and I will
not walk about, oblivious of my faults, my stars and myself,
          to be mugged by Sean, a smack-head, who is being
cared for in the community. I am not about to dive into Tooting
          Baths too soon after choosing the seafood special at
The Tikka Peacock. I am lucky in that I'm unlikely to erode
          within late-in-life psoriasis or swell up from a hitherto
undiagnosed aversion to veined Lithuanian cheese.
          I'm going to die because I'm just too fucking sweet."

"What I need, Bernard, is a bit of notice;

I can't just throw this together at the last minute.
                    I mean, if you want me to
                              say it with freesias, there's an issue
                                        with weak stems.
Denise says they'll never stretch to BERNARD and are you sure
          as the last time she popped her head around
                              you weren't being terribly clear?

Now. The water-skiing.
                    My thighs have not been strong since the Dolomites.
                    And do bear in mind the Jubilee fiasco.
          If I couldn't stand up
                    after 14 lessons at Take-the-Plunge,
I'll have no chance after a four-course wake (including cheese)
                    and your ashes under my arm.

Are you headlong on Berlioz?
          I'm not trying to split hairs
                              in your last hours but I have to tell you,
                    for most of us, *March to the Scaffold* is tricky and
                              we'll need a pick-me-up
                    with Stuart and Audrey
                              bringing Marion from Stevenage.

Did you flutter, Bernard? Did Berlioz hit a nerve?
          I don't have a preference and it is your funeral.
                    I just wish,
                    I wish we had longer to look at the menus.
          I know you feel cheated by a finger buffet
but it's only worth the trek if people can
                    rub shoulders with old friends.

And I'm sorry, but sequential seating has a whiff
of Harvest Festival.
Bernard?
I'm going to hold your hand now.
This is like the old days. Remember the picnics?
You always forged ahead with your spy-nocs to find the perfect spot,
said you wouldn't risk detritus spoiling our cold cuts.

Your hands were always fresh and cool,
rather like ham, Bernard, rather like
a nice tinned ham.
Neat and square.
Unlocked with a silver key."

Lizard

The wife of a retired dentist from Antwerp
cooks chicken on Sundays. In November
she brings out V-neck sweaters
that protect him from chest infections.
He will choose the light grey and may not remember
which of the teal or the red he last wore.

The wife of the retired dentist
prepares soup from the gizzard,
adds thyme and two leaves from a bay
that grows by the gazebo.
He pulled the cutting on holiday;
a week by the Aubette or the Alzette.

The dentist remembers a garden, or a hotel.
A man, Pierre perhaps or Philippe,
nodded and told how the green from that tree
would be sweet and the sharp white berries
should be dried. *Lay them in layers of paper, keep
them clean and warm. Monsieur, all will be well.*

The wife of the retired dentist from Antwerp
sees his face rise to the sun. His round eyes are resting,
almost smiling, thinking of plates
of pale almonds, the pastries they ate
by the roadside, on small white napkins.
Or was it soft cheese, fresh and shining with whey?

There was a terrace of cracked creamy slabs;
some stone of the region. And didn't he lean on a carving
as they spotted canoes, cutting
straight lines through curves in the water?
A dozen boys from Cadiz; a party
of cadets perhaps from *l'Académie.*

They pitched on boards, crouching with cold
their hands reached up to a bar
fixed to the side of the boat. *Ici.*
Tiens. Ici. Attention, mes fils!
Up they went and over, the river poured
from their hair, their eyes and their lips. *Arrêtez! Encore! Encore!*

The wife of the retired dentist
watches three inches of lizard. So fine, it is almost
a crack in the rock. She considers the stillness
of her left hand. The lizard nudges and catches the heat.
It stares from eyes that are endless, circled
in white. Quick as a spot, it changes its skin from smoke
to black to sand. A pulse is the smallest
                                        tick-tock, tick-tock.

There is nothing sudden about it;
this is not where I want to be

It starts when a waiter
        watches me
                look down as though a meteor
lies burning through the tablecloth.

He introduces himself as *Franco*,
            rolls his name like a conjurer, pulls out a napkin
                so fast I am sure he has
                          injured himself,
        fear the red linen will splash me,
    mark me in a way I do not want to be marked.
                        Not here.
In three white bowls of warm water,
            slices of unpeeled lemon
                cling to the surface.
I do not understand anything on the menu.

I have read it three, perhaps four times.
        This is where we go for tapas and I know now
            this means 'lid'.
On this night, words are thin shapes
            black, hanging and ridiculous.

French beans. Catalan ham.
            Ogen melon. Private Functions.
    The wine list is padded,
        wrapped and buttoned in dark leather.

Gilt chairs hang about on spindly legs
        against a burgundy darkness of some velvet.
    ~~Was it curtains or cushions?~~

I try to stop myself running
                    back there, to the room
                            with hissing door hinges and clear tubes.
        That sound is not the breath of life to him
                                any more than it is to me.

That noise has become our song,
            the reason we know where we are.
                            That's why people have songs isn't it,
                to take them to the same place at the same time?

I wonder. Would it seem somehow awkward
                    or out of place to slide across the floor,
            over the veined cream tiles, avoid the three-legged barstools,
                                push the impossible glass door,
                    pause at the astonished face
                                of the girl who takes coats, to explain:
            "Tonight, I cannot eat calamari,
                                    tonight I cannot taste chorizo.
                I don't care that the tortilla is fresh, layered
                    with onion and absurdly yellow.

I know the aubergines are smoked and the toasted halloumi,
                                spread with a deep concasse
                    was once a Moorish delicacy.

Put my coat away, or put it on,
                throw it into the street.
                            I don't care. My father never liked it.
            He is dying; he is dying, dying tonight. He may even be
                                        doing it now."

South Shore House, Long Island

Now the man who does the garden
has stopped gardening. Each Thursday he drifts
through the hothouse, composting silence.
His cash-in-hand drips home to Peru to feed
his sister and her children, Ana and round Amparo.
The youngest lives in an iron bed
on the longest, thinnest tubercular ward.
He will see them next year and waits without complaint,
sleeping his lunch hour in the coolness of the arbor
while the filthy cleaner flicks about your desk.
There'll be ash under your chair and white musk
between the cushions. She checks empty
drawers and drops damp family secrets.
I pick them off and forget them.

The foxes are back tonight
savaging the trash, nosing the scent of bones.
Perhaps the ribcage of a roast.
Egg boxes, sticky with protein.
They find nothing, but I hear
their icy sex and cannot shake them.
One is injured; his eye reflects
a single bulb from the not quite busted light.
Rime hangs on his breath.
Lightly, he lifts a front leg. Up.
Slowly down. Up. I watch the dark space
between us, feel the fog
settle back. We are again separate.
I am not afraid of being alone.
I am alone because I am not afraid.

I know I've gone too far when I think of papardelle with broccoli

It comes on just under a minute later that I miss you; that hollow feeling
when I remember you're not here.

I have to go downstairs, cook flat, yellow ribbons made almost too long
with OO flour and eggs

from Puglia chickens, enjoying themselves and, I hope, walking through
fat fields where the grass is

tough and rich, almost deliberately salted from the Adriatic that silently
seeps into the land just there.

I bathe the noodles in fontina, melted into crème fraîche and think
how you called it sour cream.

It doesn't matter and would not matter to you that you didn't
like this dish, but even as I warm

your favourite bowl, I smile at my final stab, add purple sprouting
broccoli, diagonally cut.

You might like the colours, the way the steam holds the flavour,
of Alpine milk and the bitter

black pepper that falls in so many pieces like sand or gravel or ash.
I think we're OK for salt and I'll

keep the idea of fine fresh thyme, a splash of hock or just nutmeg
and/or butter for next time.

There is so much to be said and, on the surface, most things are left unsaid

I didn't think you got John Ashbery and
            what was wrong at the buffet?

I have found him. Just that. Found him and surely no-one else
            talks of the river of life and leaves it there.

I thought we agreed he's a pretentious wanker and
            I thought someone said you looked dreadful.

When Ashbery's painter decides the subject remains a prayer,
            well, it's a closer thing than purity.

Now it's John does this and John says that. It's like I don't know you.
            For God's sake, stop glowing.

I want to run down some steps in a navy moleskin coat, a caramel scarf,
            a beret pulled down on one side, my left side.

It didn't used to be like this. Why do you say there should be more room?
            I have no room for anything.

I was so bright about you, my songbird. Now, I no longer pretend
            I know which way is upstream.

Mirror, Signal, Manoeuvre. Mirror, Signal

for JNM

I leave then for Cornwall, pretend the road is straight.
Past Stonehenge, I think of that documentary
(or was it a radio thing) about substances
found on and underneath fingertips.

We've achieved what standing still for 4,000 years has not.
By touching the stones, they're eroding; eroding and alone,
roped off with just a few stragglers staring up.
I want to say they're Japanese but they're not.

They're wet and shining, shining and pointing
towards the circle, trying to capture something.
History or stillness or an engagement between
each other, or between the A303 and the A344.

I'd rather not stop at the Little Chef; a fox is most of the way
out of a wheelie-bin and he's not stopping.
A boy with a Mr Zero T-shirt tries to wipe my windscreen.
I mouth, *No, thanks!* And he pops up a hydrogenated finger.

Five people pour from a Punto and I know there's a joke there
somewhere. I'm so tired. It's dark as Teflon and I'm tired
of wondering if I should go back or go on.
You could be anywhere and no one knows where I am.

It's not just the underfloor heating
that makes me lie down in the kitchen

even though I know the dog
          will try to lick my face and
even though crystals of mouse bait lie
          blue and a yard from my nose.

          Our friends say they don't mind leaning
               to kiss me on each cheek and
          I say our parties have become
               tricky but more interesting.

If I stay here, we need to add hot tea
          to our list of dangerous things but
I'll leave any pretence that I'm in the way.

          I don't mind hearing your *Goodnight*,
               absorbed into overhead halogen but
          I don't enjoy feeling at right angles
               to the table we bought in Penzance.

If I stay here, I need to diversify my reading
          from boxes of All-Bran, although
I'll leave the Webster's on your side of the bed.

          I try to vary the time I sneak off to the study
               to lift the Black Watch rug, although
          I try to fix the times I wake to carry it back,
               holding its folded smell of sleep.

If I stay, I'd like to discuss the large green tent
          two-thirds of the way down the garden.
If I leave, please furnish it with two striped chairs.

          After we sleep there, we might learn to see
               each other through windowless nights.
          After we wake there, you might start to talk to me
               in the language you speak in my dreams.

Morning, after moving to the rental in Pasadena

Sunday, around seven and the day spreads itself
thin. It's light, light enough to watch
as the garden unfolds. The lilac here –
it's not out. March and it's just a twist
of buds and twigs. No sign of colour or
anything familiar. I sit at that horrible
table. I know, I said I'd replace it and I will.
It's barely big enough for a book or a cup.
Not both. It's waiting, no, standing around.
There's a label, a smallish cream label
of string and red ink. *Leave - Kitchen.*
One of the legs is short, out of line
and look – the top is marked. Feel small
lines, rough on the surface.
I wonder if they cooked for each other, the people
who lived here. Did they slice shallots
or small brown mushrooms?
Perhaps they miss it, this table.
Maybe they are standing in a clearer day
than this, backs bent from unpacking,
a right hand on a hip, trying to think back.
That damn table. They might picture it
at this window, in this other sunlight -
the label trying to weave a breeze.
I may find a place for it. Tomorrow.
Or Tuesday. In a while, maybe. In a while.

The idea of buying a hat for you was much nicer
than the hat I would have bought for you and

telling you that I had a seedling idea of buying a hat for you
was nicer still than the idea of buying a hat for you and even

nicer than this was wondering if I should tell you that I had
thought of buying a hat for you when really I feared

that we did not know each other quite well enough for me
to think of telling you that yesterday I thought of buying

a hat for you because in fact I had only looked at 2 or
3 hats for you and neither of these seriously cemented

the idea that I might or might not be in a position to either
choose a hat for you or confide my idea of what a hat for you

might be although if I were to either think of buying a hat for you
or feel close enough to tell you that I thought of buying

a hat for you it would be the dove grey and not the midnight blue
that best fits my idea of a hat that might be the ideal hat for you.

Chorinho

As the band winds down, the young Pandeiro
        moves his hands around his head,
                flexes them up and out to the light.
    You know, I expected this walk to fix everything, but
      even now I don't go straight home.

A few families sit around like spoons,
        the softness in their words mixes with sounds
      of the evening, the heat and the beach.
They smile into small jugs of oranges
          floating in sweet, spiced wine.

A handful of children dance on the sand,
          curious of the change in their parents,
        careful to hold the unexpected hours by the water.
          They hide yawning eyes, their fingers
                 play in their hair.

"Limão! Baunilha! Moranga!"

The ice-cream vendor stands back,
        holds out a sherbet for the smallest.
         She leans against the cart,
        wipes pink sugar water on her dress.

The mandolin player bends himself slightly
         towards the seven-string and back
          to the clarinet.
      The old Cavaquinho sits, stares at the music
        as though seeing it for the first time.

His lips move as he speaks to each note,
        taking time to enjoy the echoes of imperfection
      between the Chorinho and the ocean.
         Finally I relax into the night, into the warm
         aluminium of my chair.

The Limit of Perpetual Snow
(Nevis, WI)

for KGB

Morning comes on with three or four boys in the kitchen.
They've been here a while, talking high, gentle, throwing
thin soursop slices one to the other, their sweet hands
stretched out, laughing as the yellow fruit slips and drops
to the grey teak floor. The cook barks and his eyes roll.
"Pull the shutters! Is the syrup on the tables? Juice, boy?"

"Too early for the butter, Clovis, do you see the sun, boy?"
This is the best time; the smells and sounds of the kitchen.
Coconut trees creak and fan out from the night, hot rolls
rest while the shift girls gather toast cuts in baskets, throw
gold crusts to Bananaquits. They love the sugar, never drop
one piece, when they fly up like blue and yellow hands.

Cook wipes his face with the back and front of his hands.
One foot on a green corn can, he smiles in the shade as a boy
comes out of the cool room, carries thick white bowls of drop
scones and plates of cut fruit. The girls reach into the kitchen,
hold doors for each other with one foot, white cloths thrown
over their shoulders. Violet covers rows of golden sweet rolls

and together we take in the ocean, take in the impossible rolls
of white horses on blue, the slowness of beach weed, my hand
as I lean from the pontoon to gather smooth stones and throw
one then another. Violet smiles, heads for the heat, the boys,
their games, the girls, their laughter, the cook and the kitchen.
She knows I'll stay here to skim stones in the sun. One, drop.

One, two, three, drop. Inside the reef, a pale blue boat drops
anchor, the crew spreads out to reel in sails. A girl swims, rolls
with the keel, then hangs on the ropes and calls to the kitchen.
One by one the boys come out, holding juice jugs in one hand,
they crinkle their eyes and laugh in the wind. The young boys
who came here from Spain? They thought part of the sky threw

white on the mountain, like snow. They tried to climb up, throw
perpetual snow into the heat of the island, where the red drops
of Flamboyant cover crumbling plantations, where girls and boys
gather bunches of blossoms, wrapped with Hibiscus and rolls
of palm leaf. These small flower parcels became gifts, handed
to friends like chicken with beans and rice from the kitchen.

I love the sounds of the kitchen, the throwaway chatter, the boys
and their games. I love the girls and the scent of sweet raisin rolls.
I love to watch bright drops from the sea, vanish into my hand.

Afternoon tea at your house
is the otherness I've been chasing

for ME and LS

There was a time when the poems I wrote
                    had sugar heaped into every line
        Refined ideas on the origin of Turbinado were
                ruinous for pre-menopausal digestion
Volcanic crystals from Demerara incited swings in mood swings
                        The fine oily sand my ancestors
        distilled in Port Louis was a recipe for melancholy or
            melancholia   whichever is stronger

Despite a certain viscosity and tick-tack stickiness
                    nothing stuck until your cerulean walls took
        my breath away and the white   white sugar
                you poured on the fire gave it back and tiny oranges
                    on painted plates released sweet oil
        their leaves curling in three different greens

I can still feel my heavy boots too heavy
                    on your butterscotch floor and
        the ambient temperature
                of your house that is not ambient but
generous and holds its separate scent
                        Lemon verbena
        Stephanotis oil
            Arabica beans

In deference to the weather
                    I chose the Penguin Classics cup
    with small-shouldered Ellis Bell etched in magenta
        This despite my ambivalence toward poor
inclement Cathy who was unable or unwilling to manage
                    anything larger than a kitten and nothing smaller

I am unused to feeling as warm
                          as my oiled Aran sweater feels without me in it
           But when you built a fire with uneven creamy logs and dotted
                          careful coal pieces like strong oily truffles
              my hands became still and I sat feline and far back
         in your uneven velvet chair
                          my feet tucked under me as if I had known
              all this for years
     The pale grey wink of Georgian windows
                          The standing stillness of your Winter pergola
           The gentle slope of your ceiling and the boiling
                          sugar spinning threads through the grate
              patterning the patterned hearth in oily pools
         transformed at last into something clear

Night fishing

I know a woman who cries at night,
                        says all kinds of things,
            like the next time her husband goes night fishing
                she'll lock him out.
I want to tell her that she will be shut in,
                      only her face gets sort of shut up too,
              jammed and so far past crying
like the door to the beach house that swelled up that Winter.

You remember, don't you?
          How we couldn't get it open till we eased out the hinges,
                    how rusted they were,
              sealed with crystals of salt and flaked steel.

One of the bolts had shorn right off but for the life of me,
                  I couldn't see where it had fallen.
          Perhaps, and I want to think this, it rolled away
              through the threads of your mother's rag rug,
        slipped down through the maple boards
            among hot water pipes,
       a tangle of line, a salmon fly
hooked around a sand dollar,
            the skeleton of a sea horse.

After a house fire in Hounslow

Indira hesitates. Asks me to go with her. Her home is smoking.
    Still. Smoking. Her shoulders fall under a groaning.
A splitting that is almost movement. An adjustment. An attempt
to cool a few joists. Bring a door or newel to a temperature
where a hand might rest. A black space is no longer a room.
    Floorboards strain. The downstairs has burst through.
The wood is left. Interrupted. Irrevocable. Someone has sprayed
a name in red. One wall is not black. A long joiner's nail waits.
It snags the hand of a fireman unwise enough to linger. My scarf
    avoids brushing the walls. Corridors. Anything. We shrink
from a bedside table. The skeletal strangeness of a child's kite.
    We cannot miss the missing roof tiles. The frame of a skylight.
Hot, wet dirt moves around our coats. For the longest minute Indira
    is alone. She shakes her head at the moon's unkindness.

A pink pencil case and a bottle of orange drink;
the fibres of 2 red felt pens

it was when the builders came to take down the scaffolding and the man
        who does the garden started hammering a new fence post
                and the milk float made its little electric noise
it was then the phone started its trill-trill thing and I know that happens
        4 seconds before the batteries run out but I picked up
                just in time for you to tell me what happened

you must have been bored to go into the field behind the house and
        in front of the wood where boy (and girl) scouts used to
                camp and be trained in the art of isolation and
you must have walked a ways to uncover a bottle with just a little
        left in it and a pencil-case with half the zip torn out and
                2 lidless red pens chewed at both ends and

you wondered if you should call the police and I congratulated
        myself for not asking why and what on earth would you say?
                I knew you were enjoying the runaway horror as
you wondered about a child dragged up to the black woods across
        uncut, dog-shit fields and perhaps given a
                drink of something sweet before

she or he unzipped that pencil case and gazed at the grazing cows
        and you mentioned that your delicately disengaged neighbours
                deterred you from involving the local force as this
he or she said might smack of the extreme and in so saying they
        cemented a reputation in your eyes as people who
                mix neighbourliness with being one and

to dispose of you and your dilemma I was pleased to hear that
        rather than handing you back the ruined cloth and
                broken schoolroom cutlery they offered
to dispose of it for you and that you had done your best to
        stop thinking about it which consisted of telephoning
                me and enabling me to think of you as you try

to stop thinking about it and now I'm sitting here listening to
      my garden waste being packed into sacks and my sensitive
          milkman as he hums beautifully down the hill
to stop where the road bends west and I watch the fat
      man from the scaffolding crew as he pretends not to
          smoke in next door's gazebo and all I can think of

is a pink pencil case, a bottle of orange drink;
          the fibres of 2 red felt pens.

"Don't take drugs, Allen, get married"
The first response of Allen Ginsberg's mother to "Howl"

My mother never tells me that the president plants listening
devices in our home, or that her ex-mother-in-law is poisoning
Prometheus (the cat) with polonium; she is just plain impossible
in her own way, just as I am in mine, and you too are impossible.

And OK, she says she's convinced she's being stalked by someone
at a call centre in South East Asia and no, that's not much to go on
but I'm lucky I've never had to take trips with her on the cross-town
to see an Upper East Side therapist with a mustard stain on his trousers.

And is she so out-of-touch that nothing she says means very much?
Not like us; when I speak you listen and when you speak I listen harder.
And does she hand out precise and less-than-well-meant advice?

"If you consider me in nothing, honey, consider me in this:
Poetry won't make you thin or rich, writing just makes you a reader.
Don't mix with people of prejudice and most especially the Dutch."

Lump

She's well into her second glass before the calamari stops
      sizzling and still she's waving an empty fork and stabbing
something neither of us can see and I don't want to see.

"And so I left; slammed the door and left. That's what I did."
      I am trying to listen to *Love Is A Many Splendored Thing*.
It doesn't matter. It's always the same. Her boy is a huge lump.

She says it over and over, like no one has heard it before. He has.
      I see him later that week. Thursday maybe. Just walking
with his lumpy head down; lumpy hands in his lumpy pockets.

Poor lump. I smile at him and duck my head to meet his face.
      He half smiles a lumpy smile and shoves back into his morning.
Last month he ran onto platform 11, towards an Intercity and into

a ticket attendant from St Lucia who provided a small sweet cup
      of polystyrene tea, a telephone number and enough soothing
silence. Poor lump, I should not know this about you, but I do.
      I know this about you and you know I know and I know you do.

I can't decide if I'm
out of my depth
or out of my wits

On your peppermint sofa you sit
                        patient like a patient
    In your galley kitchen easy-cook
                rice has the white
boiled out of itself and the hinge of a self-assembly
    cupboard hangs straining and precarious
Washed teaspoons lie unwashed
                at odd angles to the kettle
                        and I can almost hear insomnia
        in your bed-socks as they pad down the simulated
                        pine floor in search of camomile
                rosehip
                        cinnamon   anything
Your eyes really are the colour of rain
        on a Mayfair windscreen
                    Nothing is admitted in this space that has no space
In the clarity of your madness you hear
                how much I want to cure you but
        my conjurer's currency
                        counts for nothing here
                You are so very ill and you don't get up
        as I walk backwards to the door
I see you sitting still patient on the patient
        peppermint of your sofa
                            The only way I can leave is quick
                                    quick   quick
        I am nearly across Hanover Square when I hear
                    the silver rattle of the chain
                the brass click of the lock

It was precisely at this point during the
amniocentisis that Dr Healey, from
New South Wales, exposed an interest

in froghoppers and a darker side to his nature

Ever seen one?
Black and red and can they jump!
One hundred times their own length.
Bloody little miracles.

This looks longer than it is and it's a sharp one; you won't feel it.

Everyone in the city has lavender, right?
Take a look at yours;
early Spring's the best time.
It's symbiosis really.

See the monitor? Baby moves away from the intrusion. What a pro.

The nymphs drink the lavender sap;
much more than they need.
They blow the rest out of their arses.
Cuckoo spit, see?

Asshole at 10 o'clock. Anaesthetist in from Melbourne. Stay still.

The nymph's protected
from all sorts of nasties.
Less of a picnic for the host,
but that's life.

That's you two done. I only need a teaspoon.

You're not like my wife:
she's forever
talking and moving
at the wrong time.

In a bad TV show, the CIA men think
they're poets; in a good poem
the poet works for the CIA

It occurs to me on the train, on the way back
        from one of our disastrous lunches,
that the Bollinger glow in your eye might be
        just that – a Bollinger glow in your eye.
And that, because there is nothing smaller
        than your pinhole pupils, not much light
is getting in there; to your retina I mean.
        Did you know the windows of your
apartment have the capacity to look both ways?
        Did you know that letting in a greener
day than this might involve re-oxygenation or
        (at the very least) respiration?
And yet I see you still and still I see you in that
        baroque chair in your hideous room,
unable to understand the strains of Stravinsky,
        unwilling to comprehend the role
of the Vatican in the holocaust, uncompromising
        in your determination to remain undisturbed.
That disequilibrium is unrelenting, almost circular.
        Like the poet who frets that she isn't;
like the detective who thinks he is.

Perfect, private things have imperfect, public endings

i.m. Weldon Kees

And did you choose those friends with care and intelligence and did
they rinse your socks, let out the pinkish water and find a good home
for your cat whose name, I know, is Lonesome? I've read that suicides
prepare themselves with excruciating care; seldom leave errands for
others and yes, I remember they remove their glasses, sometimes
watches and also shoes. They do not tend to empty savings accounts;
usually they eschew talk of starting afresh, anew or anything ridiculous.

I hope your mind has ceased to flap like a broken blind; perhaps it was
broken. Perhaps it is. It may be dawn before you sleep and the silence
of these altered rooms has thinned. I like to think you are there now,
sitting in a different porch-light, where the wind doesn't rush and tall
angular trees are actual and take no holiday. The music will start again
inside a small responsive smile. For a while anyway, let this be enough.

After the new toaster broke itself

for JJS

I want to say   long   blue sparks flew and
a fat   raisin-jammed bagel
                        welded itself to 31 individual
                                        filaments.

I want to say it   was the same day my ring fell
            down the sink.   Not the ring I unwrapped
        after 10 years.   Two children.   Lunch.

            It wasn't the large topaz or the thin
                            gold band, randomly
            spotted with seed pearls.

It was   the morning   the fish died   and I would
        like to say its feathery   tail started to
                        wilt as it gracefully
                reduced   its hold on its
                    surroundings   leaving
            Cornish gravel   a submerged pagoda
                    four glass walls.

No.   The innards of the new toaster   collapsed when
        I jimmied a bbq fork   back and   forth to
                        retrieve the slice of granary too stiff to eat
                            without heat.
                If I'd made fresh bread   this would not
                    have happened.

I bought the lost ring   as my father sat
                in the corner of a George Town jeweller   convinced
        the CIA and the DVLC were   after him
                convinced the sun   bouncing
                        between boats in the
        harbour would blind   his eyes and melt   his skin.

48

The fish   jumped from his unkempt tank and landed
  on the black   onyx counter
  The scaled side of him moved up then down
  as his red gills tried to   pull something
      from the air   perhaps just
   some sense of things.

If I call this Umberto's darkest hour,
it is because that is precisely what it is, believe me

Umberto McGuire doesn't mind the damp
        feeling its way to his buttocks, through the uneven
            twill of his trousers,
from the bench by the glasshouse in Trinity Gardens.
        He doesn't hear the top D sharp of the noon whistle
          or the bell in the clock tower sound out his lunch hour.

At four-thirty, lamplighters filter through East Gate.
        In waxed hats and green coats, they call out their numbers,
          check the lakeside for spooning couples, lead flat Winter boats
under cover, loop stray dogs or those that look like trouble.

        Umberto McGuire, still as you please,
          whispers admonitions from St Paul's epistle.
   To mourn the departed mocks the glory of the life hereafter.
Mary McGuire loved Umberto, Queen's Choir and cooking frittata.

I start to understand yellow

i.m. Grand-maman

when I unfold your recipe for soufflé; feel the sweet brittle paper.
    Rosehill, Mauritius, 1938. These ingredients are not possible.
Verna lemons, Suffolk eggs. It's all right. I understand; only the sugar
    made sense on the plantation between Floreal and Beau Bassin.

Some said Grand-papa loved the east of the island and the stretch
    of water facing Rodrigues, across the Arabian Sea to Goa.
It all started there with his curious, grey-eyed mother.

Others said he was a bastard who pissed it all away in a poker shack
    with a mulatto woman from north west of Souillac.
No one told her when he burst through the windscreen of his Jensen
    on a skin-full of Green Island, when the moon was less than.

For fourteen nights she sat with a bundle of children, on a grass hill
    outside Floreal and each night Grand-maman passed silver
casuarinas, holding a warm clay dish of chicken and cardamom rice.

My milkman comes from Sarajevo
and has beautiful hands

and he leans against
the door frame and asks   have I ever
read Wislawa Szymborska?
He says I should not concern
myself with questions on the nature and
variation of translation
but hints that the Irish
have the best
the best ears in the business
for the swings and falls in cadence

As he passes me Cornish butter and cheese
I ask   was it not the Welsh who
most easily detect the ambient
musicality overlooked
in speech that is touched by Silesian?
He lifts cold
wet glass bottles
from a red box with partitions

Yes the Welsh have a way
with Baltic idioms and
also classical Spanish

He recalls the vowels of a young teacher
from Criccieth who visited his school
She unpacked thin volumes of Neruda and Cavafy
left over perhaps from a love affair

As my milkman from Sarajevo
hands me a dozen farm eggs
with an unsteady hand
he reflects on her complexion
how a colour gathered then vanished
just beneath her almond eyes

                        as she moved without pausing
            from Mandelstam

                            to Akhmatova and the milkman
my milkman   he says he feels Akhmatova
            close by him sometimes reciting
                                Requiem and *Poem Without a Hero*
            in the original   in deep black sea vowels
"I mourn for the terrible ghost that

                            pretends to be my city."

I must lie down where all ladders start
– WB Yeats

And did she stand on riverbanks and know
                              just where to fish?
          Did she know the streams?
                              Their names and why?

Did she feel the difference
                    between water and flow?
          Did she understand the source
                              may not always be the start?
It was not for these things I loved her; I just loved her.

Did she know the best way to light a fire was
                              while talking not looking?
          Did her square hands feel and find the way
                              to draw smoke through a flue?
Did she understand how low an ember can go
                    and still ignite its flame?
And I loved her for these things and I loved her.

Could she separate the anemone
                              from the not quite ink of her heart?
          Did she understand the silver inside rosemary needles
                              and say it just as she saw it?
Could she show me the difference
                    between grass and leaves of grass?
It was not for these things I loved her; I just loved her.

Could she explain inevitability
                              in the fermentation of pippins?
          Could she see *between-pie* as the not quite space between
                    a mountain, the earth and an almost perfect sky?
Could she feel the weight of iron and feathers?
          And I loved her for these things and I loved her.

Did she tell me that a ghost story might be a love story
                              rolled inside an unremarkable Cairo carpet?
        Was she sensitive to mythical blue pigments
                          within glazed Middle Eastern china?
            Liberty. Ultramarine. Midnight.
        It was not for these things I loved her; I just loved her.

Vanishing act

Like the drunk poet who roams the Left Bank
                    thinking he's on to something
          if he can only find it
                    I'm trying to find you after all this (I'll just say) time.
What matters is the afterglow that glows
                    after us and not the convection that
                                        ran between us.
          The place I left that thought of you, or
something that felt or looked like you, is now a laundromat.
                    It might be called *Washed Away* but it's likely
                              I made that up.
                    Looking for you was not my smallest mistake.
That place, imprinted so tight on my mind,
                    I know it cannot exist.
          The old oak bench gimped with crows' feet and shit.
                              My memory won't permit anything but
fairy lights and fiery nights – a stroll through Montparnasse.
                    The beauty of young Albanians
          spilling from keyhole bars
                              in clouds of insurrection and sweet pastis.
I felt you close just then
                              or imagined I did.
          Perhaps the only thing I have
                    is the imagination to feel close to you.

A seedy narrative or moments of lyrical stillness?

for LI and SP

A stationery salesman seizes a little extra with
a girl on a summer job in Healthy Snax. You may
consider this anticipated but, you see, he did not
plan to look twice at the pale pink of her easy-wash

overall. And his hand did not intend to brush hers as
she counted his 17p change. But maybe she surprised
him by licking her finger to select a small bag for his
Mexican wrap, pre-packed date slice and grape crush.

Did she experience a premonition of Room 149 at
the Ramada Hotel, just off the Ring Road? Did she
feel a gathering, only that morning as her brothers
jostled like beagles, shovelling toast down the path?

Perhaps he lingered over 2-nights pre-paid or maybe
her pulse quickened at the inclusion of a lemon wedge
in the Friday Fish Special. I'd like to think she paused
at some unexpected warmth. Was it the peach towels?

The sweet circular soap? A delicacy in the afternoon
light from the fly-over? Did she lift the single mint-
chocolate from her pillow, break it in two and save
each half for some tender moment, later?
Much later.

I prefer training personally to being personally trained

OK, I'm cheating.
      I know how this turns out, only not
            like dinner reservations or Summer plans
    or the pollen from that July flower that we
                  agree stinks of cats.
I've decided to give you up and not for Lent.
      Remember when I opened a bottle of mirin?
            Explained that this is Japanese rice wine vinegar?
The next bit was lost in the translation of our
                uncommon language.
You see, flavour
      any flavour becomes sour and more inhibited
            by your need to utilise the luminous blue
    shelf of your enormous built-in
                Norwegian fridge.

Conversations concerning Brownian motion
      intrigue me and bore you. I guess I'm
            fascinated by things that move without
    definition. Like the cloud of pizza dust
                in the air near the subway.
It's just, just there, floating in the
      lightest understanding of still-warm disconnections;
            like the air vents outside the Dakota.
They have their own temperature that defies
                measurement.

I know you'll try to pin this down, establish
      consensus on the nature of things. You won't understand and
            you won't listen; solutions are no solution.
    Their construction is an excuse to stop thinking.
                Stop talking. Stop.

Constantly risking absurdity
—Lawrence Ferlinghetti

I have been stamped in the untruth of your hard-beam
       headlights and I remind myself of the sharp flavours
            sights and the sharpest thoughts
      to enjoy within the warmer universe of your absence

You are in no danger of mistaking anything
       for what it isn't   Nor are you within
            the closest approximation to the vivid
      empathy you deploy to box me
              into a brown circle of the suburban

And I did love the idea of loving and being
       loved by you and I did enjoy the gentle
            effervescence of that cloudy organic wine and
      yes I confess to a communion with the buzzing
             of that delightfully failing neon sign

You, super realist, have damned me
       for knowing too much and in separating the hairline crack
            stopped-watch sense of me and
      by folding up both of us you have removed each of us

When it ends I will live only
       in my recollection of present tense events
            Ended I will start to eclipse even
      the darkest unbidden but not hidden parts of you.

The morning I reverse my BMW over your necklace is just another
morning

The man who walks sideways across the zebra
                    crossing is finishing his little crab shuffle.
   It starts to drizzle and he greets cars face on, opening and closing
                    his black hole mouth to catch fat spots of grey.
   He thanks every driver and smiles up to my window.
                    I raise my pale blue cup to him.
         He's happy and I decide to run over your necklace.
                    I will wait till he's gone.
He is happy and he will not understand when I lean
                    quietly and carefully to lay the long
      string of Mikimoto pearls behind my back wheel.
                    Passenger side, I think, and wonder what will break first.
Perhaps one of the beautifully imperfect spheres
                    will compress or shoot
      off at an impossible angle to injure a pigeon, but not
         a linnet and not the wren I heard and have
                    not heard since Tuesday.

         I'm betting the thread will snap first and
      I bump into a bin man as he leaves
                    my recycling in thin orange bags that lean
into a sour breeze and half a sun.
                    A velvety tray (that held 2 Victoria plums)
      squeaks between a Manolo Blahnik box and a white
                    takeout bag from the Good Earth.
As I move my car in a long slow arc, there is no noise;
                    no snap like a hock glass on marble.
   The sky does not darken and the sideways man does not hurry back.
                    I'm a third of the way around
Beaufort Square when I consider pedestrians
                    passing the mess of beads and bead pieces.
      Perhaps mothers will hesitate, hold back
                    their toddlers from the glitter,
now mixed with grit from the street.

Will a magpie even try to resist
                    pecking at the sharp, broken whiteness?
At the dry-cleaners, clear plastic covers wrinkle up
                    in my face. I pay for 1 cashmere cardigan,
1 sage silk dressing gown, 2 evening dresses. One is black; the other not.
                    Everything is slowing down too fast.
The hygienist is running late. The butcher is talking
                    to someone in a brown van.

My car is waiting; loudly waiting to take me home, to search for
                    surviving beads, take them inside, choose
        a string or ribbon in green silk or black
                    cord or a fine gold chain.
Will it hang to my ribs? Or nest in the heat
                    just below my throat? Perhaps I will
        divide them with a random handful of amber or
                    a dizzy of amethyst.
Maybe I should leave them in the tiny glass bowl that
                    sits on the circular table, to the right of my bed.
        From there, the noon sun
                    reaches my luminous ruin,
    sends light through half a dozen
                    unexpected colours that cannot quite separate.
    See them dance from the window to the ceiling and down the walls.
                    The day is quieter now.

2 out of 12 organic eggs are cracked;

I feel you might have had a hand in this.
And by the way, these groceries are disastrously packed.

Meat juice in the icing sugar forms a dozen specks
        or blobs of brownish red, congealed in sucrose mist
and 4 of 12 organic eggs are cracked.

Pretending to recall means trying to forget
        the order of things, although it's pretty hard to miss
these disastrous groceries I guess you must have picked.

3 croissants, 5 peaches; for God's sake just accept
        time away from me is time you've missed
the cracks in 6 of these 12 eggs, and yes, they're black.

6 cracked, 2 smashed, 2 breaking, only 2 intact;
        hopeful handfuls, holding clear albumen mist.
They sit amidst these groceries (unpacked but not unpicked).

I wait till Sunday morning before I finally crack.
        A tiny pause to write a note that reads more like a list:
"These eggs aren't fine; they're yours and all of them are cracked.
The groceries are mine and they are beautifully packed."

I want to think you'll make a neat job
of confiscating my heart

It's up to you, but here's an idea.
It could be not dissimilar
to the removal of Anne Boleyn's head.
When he saw the neatness of her muslin cap
and the whiteness of her neck,
the executioner hesitated, called
fetch my sword to distract them both.
He dismissed her
before she could gather
anything.

I may feel foolish but I am not unwise.
Your perception of pain is not unlike garden furniture
left out past September.
It assumes infinite tolerance to seasons,
the reversible effects of corrosion,
the garrulous nature of slugs.
I know your concentration will be
dipping now,
so before you start, I promise:
There will be no untidiness and it will make
almost no noise.

Nature is the poetry of evidence;
poetry is the evidence of nature

(i.m. Dr Rosalind Franklin, who first photographed the double helix.)

And I wonder, did you hide a fear
of looking down, reaching down into that
emphasis that is almost

italicized? Perhaps you felt the hairs on your neck
form their own diffraction of
a day running parallel to

itself. As the soft part of your hand curled,
the darkness of your eyes disbelieved and believed
itself into an evening of exacting

stillness. Your strength and the strength of any code
lies in the visibility of its invisibility.
The code between you and the helix exists

outside laboratory conditions; its nature and yours
allow messages of precision to
form a new form, an intimate

folding. Like recognition, like a message collapsing
on itself, leaving behind some scent
of another self; that weakness of hydrogen

bonds. It is not weakness but vital for replication,
vital for each strand to break and reform
but not to conform or

confirm. I know a word exists to describe the
symbiosis between form and function, but remember
naming is just one kind of misunderstanding.

Syzygy

(A storm phenomenon where the sun, the moon and the earth align)

As Mr and Mrs Jarvis fly past the bathroom window, I realise I have
never previously seen them hold hands. He is in catering supplies.

She fiddles with crochet (that mostly resembles a cat's-cradle rainbow) and
waits for the crunch of 6:30 and the rumble of the Rover in the drive.

When the storm spins them tight like a bobbin, their mouths spring open
in a double O and I am sure I hear a gasp at right angles to the rain.

It skids down our roof as Mr Jarvis follows Mrs Jarvis along the gutter,
their faces drained of colour, her all-weather mac blown out in a parade.

He wears tan driving gloves and puts one hand on his wife's left arm.
She holds his finger in one of her mittens, the one with a lime green run.

With some shyness, they peep just inside the second floor of our house.
Mrs Jarvis, who goes out of her way to be friendly, smiles and waves

to Brian, our plumber, as he recalibrates both gauges on the boiler.
Mr Jarvis nods, looks at his wife, then over her shoulder at the clouds

lining the unexpected sky and, at a distance, I see surprise in their eyes.
They laugh at the same time as their arms struggle, then join in a circle,

their shoulders suddenly sure how to bend towards each other, to be
together, at once aligned, even if this is not really, quite, the end.

Anchorman

(for Guillermo José Torres, TV commentator on Karl Wallenda's
fatal high wire walk – San Juan, Puerto Rico, 22nd March, 1973)

Your anguished cry circled the world
as 74-year-old Karl Wallenda made a grab
for the wire, tried to find the wire,
that wire; distinguish it from the wind.
That wind followed him everywhere.
All his life. All his life, he followed the wire and the wind
followed him from place to place. To place.
Philadelphia. Tallulah River. King's Island.
Such an unremarkable man; up there. Up.
There. He might have been
an ageing bookkeeper.
Thirty years 9 to 5 and still
the junior man on the pole.
He might have climbed out of his office
window to walk across the sky to see
a woman in the next building.

There she is, the one with dark hair that
moves as she walks,
moves in that same warm
wind from the Torrid Zone.
Into the Torrid Zone he walks in his
ballet-black slippers.

Perhaps he might ask her out
for a cheeseburger, a movie or maybe
a stroll in the park, the one with
the beautiful name, the park where people stretch
on cool grass.

He had never walked there, watched sun
                  falling into and across the lake, watched
            secretaries, salesmen, off-duty firemen,
                              the man who lifts leaves.
                  Talking. Laughing. Touching.
            He never walked with someone
      and pretended, just pretended for a time that he was
                        in love and loved; that he was held.

My insomnia handbook instructs me
to select a number, then count backwards in
slow, single units, allowing tangential
images to intrude, should they facilitate sleep

33, 32, 31. Even inside out, a pillowcase can't
count backwards in singles; the curtains only count
        forwards and only in pairs. The total
acreage of my shoe cupboard is obsessed

        with walking north in multitudinous steps.
30, 29, 28. The small Viennese water glass, in its
        circular lace circle, is diminished in sips of
three or four; replenished in a motion that is defiantly

        plural. My sheets. Listen to them. Sheet(s).
They are layered and, damn them, they work
        collectively and cumulatively. 27, 26, 25.
The fireplace is black and singular; the chimney isn't.

        24, 23, 22. For every opening of my bedroom
door, there is an incomplete and opposite closure.
        21, 20, 18. Sorry. 19. This book's asking
the impossible. Turn back time. As if. 18, 17, 16.

        The sound of a fox or a cat (I hope not together)
mincing through one of the bins. The bins! The bins
        are paired and roll together down the path.
15, 14, 13. There is a man up the road who has a

        motorbike and no manners. In two hours
he will leave for his office in the city. I cannot be woken
        up if I am already awake. I will be woken up and I am
already awake. The sound of his foot hitting

        the black rubber pedal will (12, 11, 10) deafen my
brain long after he has left his smug sleeping wife, his
        ungainly comatose children. Maybe he's a counting
backwards kind of guy. Driving backwards towards

the river. 9, 8, 7. Backwards over Battersea Bridge.
Turn backwards and right along Cheyne Walk. A long,
        slow thought of him plunging, fat arse first into the
icy Thames; releasing his hold on the ridiculous black

        gloves that make him look (even more) like a Nazi.
6, 5, 4. A facilitating image of my neighbour, drowning;
        this could be working. The image of one of his black
biker boots, floating east and sideways towards

        the flood barrier. Perhaps a single stockbroker sock,
waving red bulls with blue balls in the clear green current.
        Waving and tumbling in gentle, somnolent filth
under Albert, Chelsea, Vauxhall, Grosvenor. 3, 2, 1.

Hermeneutics

I want poems that are stained
            with rings of coffee and perhaps
                  cigarette ash or a stain of oily red sauce
      hinting at a heavy-handed
                experiment in Hungarian cooking.

I want pages to be folded over
            and over until the filaments of cellulose
                lie exposed and seem almost willing
     to tear at the touch of someone who
            is not accepting of exploratory lineation.

I would like to feel the dig of a pencil or a pen in
            the shorter lines and see the longer lines lined and
                underlined in exasperated colours
    and surrounded by Cyrillic expletives that remain
            without translation.

I would like to smile or blush (perhaps both)
            when a person of practical persuasion suggests a visit
                to a manufacturer of staple guns or a weaver of
    tensile steel rope with which to bind these
            poems into a form less fluid.

I do not want poems to be part of the Dewey
            (or any other) system and I will stop eating cakes
                mid-afternoon if I find them in stock
    on Amazon or the object of an online
            bidding battle with no base price.

I would like to imagine a man throwing poems
            from a moving car on Pont Neuf
                less than half an hour after leaving
    a tragically beautiful and ultimately
                shallow girl on the east tip of Île de la Cité.

I hope poems are never a minor part of the syllabus
              in higher or what passes for the other kind
                        of education and I would pay to have them left
       out of any single-sex book group that does not
               suffer volatile swings in membership.

I remember a Russian ballerina whose technique was as
              remarkable as her temperament
                   explaining to a critic from Nottingham: *I dance
    *the way I dance not because I possess great
            understanding but because I do not.*

Acknowledgements

Thanks are due to the editors of the following magazines, anthologies and online publications where some of these poems first appeared:

Agenda, Ambit, The Bow-Wow-Shop, The Forward Anthology 2013, Hippocrates Anthology 2012, Interpreter's House, Iota, Magma, MMU Poetry Prize, The Moth, New Welsh Review, New Seminary Review (US), *The North, Poetry Ireland Review, Poetry London, Poetry Review, Poetry Wales, Rialto, The Shop, Tokens for the Foundlings* (Seren), *The Sunday Times* (Poet's Corner) and *The Warwick Review.*

'I must lie down where all ladders start' is dedicated to the family and friends of Nicky Tweedy.

Some of these poems appeared in *That-so-easy thing*, which was published by Smith/Doorstop in 2012.

I am grateful and thankful to Georgia Lee, Peter Lee, Sam Lee and Liane Strauss for their intelligence, insight, enthusiasm and irrepressible humour which are invaluable and precious.